W9-CII-548

LOCUST VALLEY LIBRARY

SCIENCE FILES

energy

SOLAR POWER

Please visit our web site at: www.garethstevens.com
For a free color catalog describing Gareth Stevens Publishing's
list of high-quality books and multimedia programs,
call 1-800-542-2595 (USA) or 1-800-387-3178 (Canada).
Gareth Stevens Publishing's fax: (414) 332-3567.

Library of Congress Cataloging-in-Publication Data

Parker, Steve.
    Solar power / by Steve Parker.
      p. cm. — (Science files. Energy)
    Includes bibliographical references and index.
    ISBN 0-8368-4032-1 (lib. bdg.) *1445984*
    Contents: Bathed in energy — Solar-powered world — Light to electricity — Power from the sun —
Smaller solar — Solar "to go" — Solar in space — Solar heat — Free heat at home — Nature's solar energy —
Second-hand solar — Solar take-over? — Future solar energy.
    1. Solar energy—Juvenile literature. [1. Solar energy.] I. Title.
TJ810.3.P37   2004
621.47—dc22   2003060562

This North American edition first published in 2004 by
Gareth Stevens Publishing
A World Almanac Education Group Company
330 West Olive Street, Suite 100
Milwaukee, WI 53212 USA

Original edition © 2002 by David West Children's Books. First published in Great Britain
in 2002 by Heinemann Library, Halley Court, Jordan Hill, Oxford OX2 8EJ, a division
of Reed Educational and Professional Publishing Limited. This U.S. edition © 2004 by
Gareth Stevens, Inc. Additional end matter © 2004 by Gareth Stevens, Inc.

David West Editor: James Pickering
Picture Research: Carrie Haines, Carlotta Cooper
Gareth Stevens Editor: Carol Ryback
Gareth Stevens Designer: Kami Koenig
Cover Design: Melissa Valuch

Photo Credits:
Abbreviations: (t) top, (m) middle, (b) bottom, (l) left, (r) right

CORBIS: Front cover (tl) and (m), 3, 5(tr), 9(tl), 6(tl), 7(tr), 7(br), 8(tr), 8(br), 9(mr),
10–11(t), 11(br), 18(m), 19(bl), 21(t), 25(mr).
Roger Vlitos: 4(t), 24–25(t), 25(ml).
Freeplay: 4(b), 17(br).
Junghans Uhren GmbH: 4–5, 16(br).
NASA: 5(br), 18–19, 6(br), 16–17, 19(tr), 30(b).
Robert Harding Picture Library: Louis Salou 9(br).
Still Pictures: Thomas Raupach 11(mr), 13(br), 28(br), 28–29(t); Mark Edwards 14(ml);
Klein/Hubert 14(mr); Dylan Garcia 14(b); Joerg Boethling 15(mr); Herbert Giradet 15(br);
Jorgen Schytte 22(tr); Mike Kollofel 23(tl); Sean Sprague 23(br).
Katz/FSP: 12–13, 13(t), 14(tr), 15(tl), 17(tl), 20(br).
Global-Merchants, USA: solar radio 16(mt), solar hat 16(mb).
Schlaich Bergermann und Partner Gbr/Stuttgart: 20(bl), 29(bl), 29(br).
Spectrum Colour Library: 22(bl), 28(bl).
ARS, USDA: 26(ml), 26–27.
Methanol Institute: 27(bl).

All rights reserved to Gareth Stevens, Inc. No part of this book may be reproduced, stored in
a retrieval system, or transmitted in any form or by any means, electronic, mechanical, photocopying,
recording, or otherwise, without the prior written permission of the publisher except for the inclusion
of brief quotations in an acknowledged review.

Printed in the United States of America

2 3 4 5 6 7 8 9 10 09 08 07 06

SCIENCE FILES

energy

SOLAR POWER

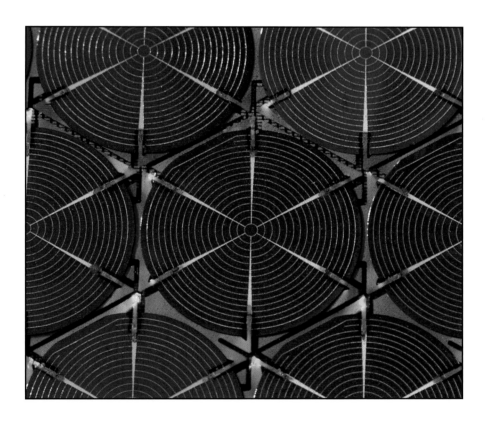

Steve Parker

Gareth Stevens Publishing
A WORLD ALMANAC EDUCATION GROUP COMPANY

CONTENTS

BATHED IN ENERGY 6

SOLAR-POWERED WORLD 8

LIGHT TO ELECTRICITY 10

POWER FROM THE SUN 12

SMALLER SOLAR 14

SOLAR "TO GO" 16

SOLAR IN SPACE 18

SOLAR HEAT 20

FREE HEAT AT HOME 22

NATURE'S SOLAR ENERGY . . . 24

SECOND-HAND SOLAR 26

SOLAR TAKE-OVER? 28

FUTURE SOLAR ENERGY 30

GLOSSARY 31

BOOKS AND WEB SITES 31

INDEX 32

All life is solar-powered. Plants catch sunlight to grow, animals eat plants, other animals eat them, etc.

A portable radio uses solar power by day, battery power at night.

Go outside and look around. Feel the heat of the Sun on your skin. That warmth is part of the energy released by the Sun — solar energy. Its light, heat, and other rays travel across 93 million miles (150 million kilometers) of empty space to reach Earth. It may seem as if we just started using solar energy to power our calculators and streetlights, but using the Sun's power is nothing new. In fact, all other energy sources, coal, oil, wind, natural gas — and even life itself — exist because of solar energy.

Solar panels contain millions of tiny electronic devices called photovoltaic cells. They change the Sun's energy directly into electrical energy.

Sunlight is strong in space. Solar panels make enough electricity for a space station.

Solar cells on the face of this wristwatch charge a battery that stores enough power to tick without light.

BATHED IN ENERGY

Our Sun is a star — a giant, burning ball in space. Every second, it produces enormous amounts of energy that radiates in all directions. Only a very tiny portion of this energy reaches Earth.

SOLAR RAYS

All the types of energy from the Sun are together called solar energy. They are mainly in the form of waves or rays, made of combined electrical and magnetic energy. These waves travel through space at the speed of light — 186,000 miles per second (300,000 kilometers per second). One of the most familiar types of solar energy is light — sunlight. Other types of solar energy you have heard about include heat, radio waves, microwaves, and X rays.

THE SUN'S ENERGY

Solar energy is also called electromagnetic radiation. The Sun's energy is produced in a spectrum — or range — of different lengths, called wavelengths.

Solar energy ranges from radio waves miles long, to gamma rays just billionths of an inch long.

Electromagnetic spectrum

Radio waves

Radar waves

Microwaves

Infrared (heat) waves

Visible light

Ultraviolet waves

X rays

Gamma rays

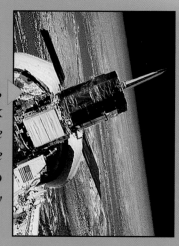

Several satellites, such as SolarMax and Helios, have traveled very close to the Sun to measure its energy

INSIDE THE SUN

Our Sun is an immense, fiery sphere 870 thousand miles (1.4 million km) across. It produces energy deep in its core at temperatures of 27 million degrees Fahrenheit (15 million degrees Celsius). This solar energy passes through the convection zone — a seething mass of swirling and burning winds — and the radiation zone to escape from the Sun's photosphere, or surface, into space.

Plants use their leaves to absorb energy from sunlight and to make energy-rich seeds and flowers. (see page 24).

Hydrogen core

Convection zone

Radiation zone

Photosphere

SOLAR FUSION

Like all stars, the Sun is made mostly of the Universe's lightest substance — hydrogen. Its center is under tremendous temperature and pressure so intense that it "fuses," or combines the nuclei of hydrogen atoms to form helium atoms and radiates huge quantities of energy into space.

Green ISSUES

Solar energy is the most long-lasting or sustainable form of energy we have, but the Sun will not last forever. In about five trillion years, the Sun will run out of hydrogen, the main fuel for its fusion. It will swell into a red giant — a larger, but cooler, type of star — then slowly fade away.

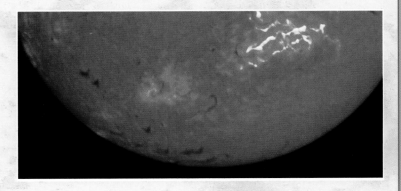

As it "dies," the Sun will swallow Earth.

7

SOLAR-POWERED WORLD

All of our energy sources come from the Sun, either directly, or through a series of energy changes.

AIR AND WATER

The Sun warms air and water. Warm air rises, and cool air moves along to take its place. This creates wind energy that we harness with windmills, sailing ships, or wind turbines.

Warm water turns into invisible water vapor, rises into the sky, cools to form droplets in clouds, falls as rain, and flows downhill along rivers to the ocean. Again, we harness the energy to run watermills and hydroelectric power plants.

PREHISTORIC SOLAR ENERGY

Millions of years ago, vast forests grew in sunlit, steamy swamps. Dead plants piled up in many layers that squashed together over time and slowly turned into coal. In a similar way, billions of tiny living plants and animals in the oceans died, sank to the bottom, got covered by more layers, and gradually changed into oil and natural gas. When we burn these three fossil fuels — coal, oil, and natural gas — we unlock stored solar energy from long, long ago.

A hydroelectric dam converts the energy of moving water to electricity.

Water cycle runs hydroelectric plant
Earth's natural water cycle, powered by the Sun, provides energy in the form of fast-flowing water.

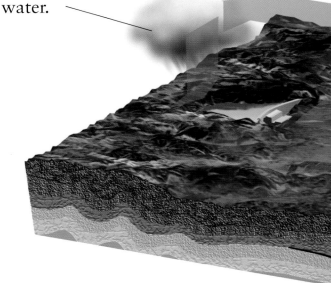

Deep in a coal mine, workers remove rock made from plants that once thrived using sunlight as energy.

The Sun radiates light and heat into our world. Various types of power plants change these energy forms, or their effects, into electricity, our favorite form of energy. Electrical energy is convenient and easy to transport long distances. We use enormous amounts of electric power daily without even realizing it comes from the Sun.

Solar panels change sunlight directly into electricity, with no in-between stage.

Solar power plants
Solar plants can trap the Sun's light, using photovoltaic cells, or its heat, using pipes or a solar furnace.

Wind farm
Rows of wind turbines gather the kinetic (moving) energy of air currents and convert it into electricity.

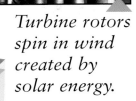

Turbine rotors spin in wind created by solar energy.

Tidal power
The Sun's pull of gravity causes about one quarter of tidal motion. The Moon's gravity causes the rest.

Fossil fuel power plant
Coal, oil, and natural gas are the remains of living things that were buried, squeezed, and heated deep in rocks for millions of years. These fossiled plants and animals contain energy in the links or bonds between their various chemicals. Burning them releases the energy as heat and light.

Coastal areas often use dams to harness tidal energy as ocean water flows into a river at high tide, then back out at low tide.

9

LIGHT TO ELECTRICITY

A solar cell is a small electronic device — about the size of a fingernail — that changes sunlight directly into electricity.

CELLS, PANELS, AND ARRAYS

A more correct name for the solar cell is the photovoltaic cell, which means it is a device that generates power (voltage) using light ("*photo*" in Greek). In bright light, a typical solar cell produces only one or two volts — about the same as a single "AA" battery. A solar panel holds many solar cells side by side, and a solar array is made of many solar panels, so the volts add up to produce useful amounts of electricity — sometimes enough to power entire cities.

Solar panels always face the direction of the strongest sunlight.

SUNLIGHT

SOLAR CELL

INSIDE A SOLAR CELL

Light travels in packets of energy called photons. When photons hit a solar (photovoltaic) cell, they excite tiny particles called electrons, freeing them to "flow" between the two layers of the solar cell. The upper layer ("p") has a positive charge, and the lower layer ("n") has a negative charge, which creates an electric field. The flowing electrons produce electricity.

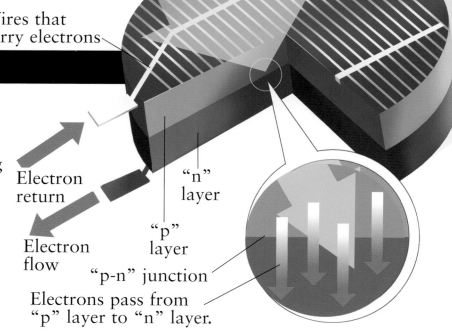

Wires that carry electrons

Electron return

Electron flow

"n" layer

"p" layer

"p-n" junction

Electrons pass from "p" layer to "n" layer.

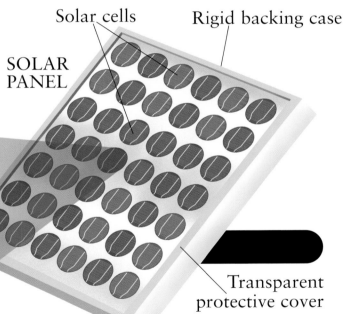

Solar cells   Rigid backing case

SOLAR
PANEL

Transparent
protective cover

*Photovoltaic cells come
in several shapes (round,
rectangular, or square),
and can have a covering
of rigid glass or plastic,
or even flexible plastic.*

Like computer microchips, solar cells
are made of semiconductors such as silicon.
Other semiconducting materials used to
make the photovoltaic cells include gallium,
cadmium, boron, and arsenic. Some of these
materials are rare, and they must be made
very pure. The processes of mining and
purifying the semiconductors require much
energy and produce various waste materials.
Some wastes might harm the environment
and must be treated to make them safe.

Solar cells require very pure raw materials.

POWER FROM THE SUN

A solar power plant needs a sunny location. Millions of tiny solar cells, arranged on thousands of panels, change sunlight into electricity.

HOW MUCH POWER?

Each day the total solar energy reaching Earth is far more than we could ever use. One-third of the Sun's energy bounces back into space. Much of the rest creates winds and drives the water cycle (see page 8). Sunlight falling on one square yard (one square meter) of Earth provides roughly 1.8 horsepower per minute — or about 1,343 watts per minute. That's a lot of power!

HOW MUCH SUN?

These maps compare solar energy arriving at ground level in different places over an entire year. The Sun's strength is greatest at the Equator.

Some regions are often cloudy, so less solar energy reaches the ground. Places such as deserts have fewer clouds — but also fewer people that could use the solar power.

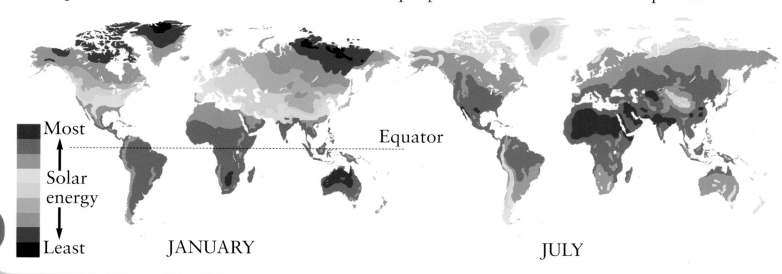

Most

Solar energy

Least

Equator

JANUARY

JULY

Controllers (inset) monitor the amounts of electricity being fed into the distribution network, or "grid." Other energy sources must "fill the gap" in the electricity supply at night and on cloudy days. A worker (left) cleans solar panels at a large solar power plant in Spain.

POWER WHERE NEEDED

Solar power is greatest in places which are sunny and hot all year. Many of these regions are very far from population areas. The process of transporting the electricity produced by a remote solar power plant to where it was needed would consume huge amounts of energy.

Green ISSUES

In order to collect enough sunlight to power a city, you would need a solar plant many times larger than that city. Huge arrays of solar panels, each containing hundreds of tiny photovoltaic cells, would take up a very large area and greatly disturb the natural environment.

The world's biggest solar power plant is in the Mojave desert.

13

SMALLER SOLAR

Solar energy varies through the day and through the seasons and can be inefficient for big power plants to use — but usage of smaller solar panels is growing like weeds!

CUSTOMIZED SOLAR PANELS

Small solar panels are now appearing in many places. Often they provide "auxillary" — or backup — power. If the Sun shines, solar panels power a light, radio, telephone, refrigerator, or other appliance, and charge batteries for cloudy times or during the night.

The Sun provides backup electricity in many places, such as fast food outlets.

Televisions need more power than lightbulbs. The main power line and batteries can also provide electricity.

Solar panels are ideal for individual, isolated power needs — such as this flashing float, or buoy, in Tarifa Harbor, Spain.

Solar panels in central Australia work better when raised above low-level dust.

14

This Japanese house collects enough sunlight for its own electricity needs — with some to spare. The owners sell extra power back to the local electric utility.

SELF-CONTAINED

Solar cells improve all the time. Older types converted only one-tenth of the light energy that hit them into electricity. In newer solar cells, this amount has more than doubled. Also, as more photovoltaic cells are made, and their designs become more established, the cost per cell falls.

Small solar panels are especially useful in out-of-the-way places that are not hooked up to a central electric supply. The panels charge batteries for "sunless" periods. Improved rechargeable batteries, better semiconductors, and other technological advances in solar energy generation all increase the practicality of solar energy use.

These University of Northumbria offices in England are designed to save on heating and lighting costs by using the Sun's energy to power some of its systems at times.

Green ISSUES

Cost-per-unit falls as more factories produce more solar panels and other solar-powered devices. Energy alternatives include burning coal, oil, or natural gas, or even bio-fuels. Burning any of these energy sources releases greenhouse gases into the air (see page 27).

Solar lamp factory, India

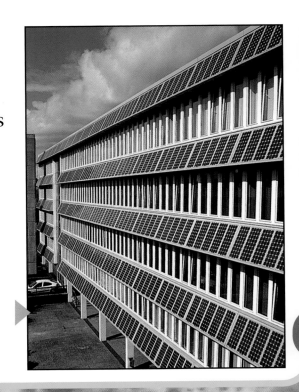

SOLAR "TO GO"

Every year, personal electronics shrink in size and weight and become more energy-efficient. Many of these devices run on solar cells that work even in dim lighting.

CONVENIENT SOLAR ENERGY

Improvements in electronics such as portable radios, laptop computers, cell phones, and digital cameras led to changes in the power sources for these personal appliances. Solar cells often supply enough power to run the devices as well as to charge any back-up batteries. Using light for power saves energy, raw materials, and reduces hazardous waste, such as disposable batteries.

Calculators and watches were among the first small, light-powered electronics. Solar panels on hats are in an ideal position to power radios and cooling fans.

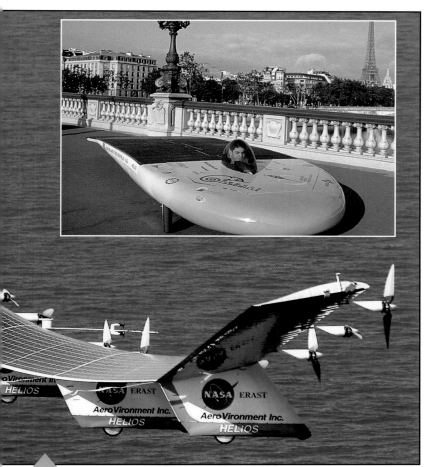

CUTTING EDGE

As solar cells become smaller, lighter, cheaper, more efficient, and easier to manufacture, inventors will find even more uses for them. Right now, many of these ideas for the use of solar power are still experimental. Remote, sunny areas far from a centralized electric power source will benefit the most from advances in solar power. New information gained from "cutting edge" solar research projects, including solar-powered vehicles such as cars, planes, and boats, will eventually trickle down to become part of everyday life.

(Inset) Experimental solar cars offer streamlined designs. (Above) NASA's Helios solar-powered flying wing, a remote-controlled, ultralightweight plane, takes a test flight over the Hawaiian Islands.

🌍 *Green* ISSUES

British inventor Trevor Baylis developed the "clockwork radio" in the 1990s. The radio works anywhere, making it cheap to use and perfect for people in remote areas. Newer versions use both solar energy and a hand-wound clockwork mechanism for power.

Solar- and self-powered radio — Zambian school, Africa

SOLAR IN SPACE

High above Earth in the emptiness of outer space, sunlight is undimmed by the atmosphere and its clouds, dust, and pollutants.

WINGS AND DRUMS

Spacecraft and satellites use solar panels shaped like wings or drums to run their cameras, computers, telecommunication links to Earth, and other equipment. Solar wings (folded for launch) extend to their full size in orbit to point toward the Sun. Solar drums spin as the satellite orbits to keep the craft's position and course steady.

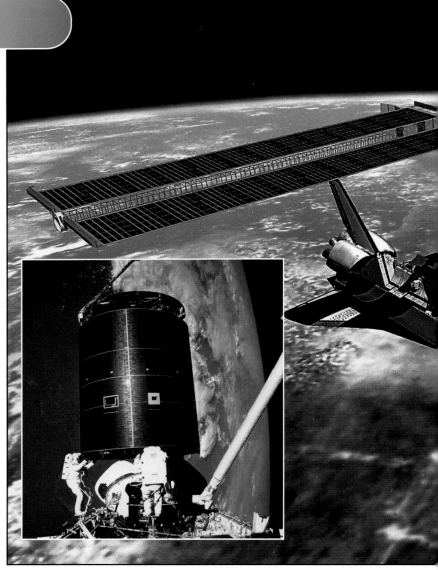

ELECTRIC WINGS

The typical suface area of a satellite's solar panels covers about 120 square yards (100 sq m). Thruster engines keep the panels facing toward the Sun.

Solar arrays

Solar panels in array

SUNLIGHT

Computer

Batteries

Thruster

Electricity

Astronauts maneuver the drum-shaped Intelsat VI communication satellite (inset), into the Space Shuttle's bay for maintenance. No matter which way the satellite faces, some solar panels are always lit.

Sojourner *was a skateboard-sized electric vehicle with a solar panel "roof." It explored Mars in 1997 and sent back many amazing photographs through radio signals.*

DAY AND NIGHT

Solar panels on Earth-orbiting spacecraft cannot face the Sun all the time, so they charge on-board batteries for times of darkness, or "night."

Deep-space craft that travel near Mars (the next planet away from the Sun after Earth) and beyond cannot use solar cells for power. These planets are too far away from the Sun and the sunlight that reaches them is so dim that solar panels do not work. Such deep-space craft usually carry a small nuclear power plant for electricity.

In a few years, after it is fully assembled, the ISS (International Space Station), *(above) will be about the size of a football field.*

Solar panels have powered the Hubble Space Telescope *(right) since 1990.*

SOLAR HEAT

Part of the Sun's electromagnetic spectrum hits the Earth in the form of infrared waves, or heat (see page 6). We can use some of that heat for power.

HEAT RAYS

Earth's Sun is a star — a massive spot in space that gives off light, heat, and other radiation. Think of it as a place where millions of hydrogen bombs are exploding all at once — continuously. All those explosions produce incredible amounts of heat. A solar furnace uses mirrors to angle and reflect (bounce) heat waves from the Sun so that they focus together at one small, very hot area.

SOLAR FURNACE

Many small mirrors tilt to track and reflect solar rays onto a huge curved mirror. This mirror concentrates its rays on a central tower to produce about 5,400° F (3,000° C) of heat energy.

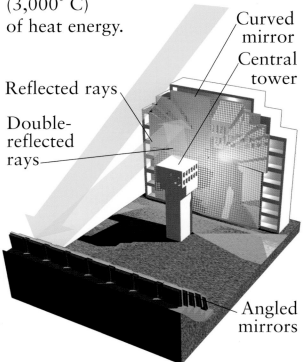

Curved mirror

Central tower

Reflected rays

Double-reflected rays

Angled mirrors

Since heat and light are the same types of waves, mirrors reflect (bounce) both of them. Curved mirrors focus, or concentrate, heat into a "hot-spot."

Sunlight reflects in the main mirror.

In a typical electric power plant, a source of heat boils water into high-pressure steam. This turns a fan-like turbine (below). In many power plants, the heat source is burning coal, oil, or natural gas. A solar furnace collects the Sun's infrared rays from a huge area by tilting mirrors which bounce the heat to a central collector on a tower. The rest of the power plant is standard.

Solar One in California has 1,818 mirrors, each 23 by 23 feet (7 by 7 m). The tower reaches nearly 300 feet (91 m).

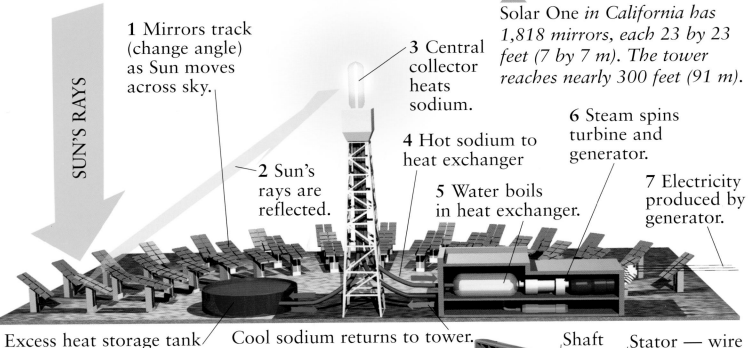

SUN'S RAYS

1 Mirrors track (change angle) as Sun moves across sky.

2 Sun's rays are reflected.

3 Central collector heats sodium.

4 Hot sodium to heat exchanger

5 Water boils in heat exchanger.

6 Steam spins turbine and generator.

7 Electricity produced by generator.

Excess heat storage tank

Cool sodium returns to tower.

Steam in

Turbine rotor blades

Used steam

Shaft

Stator — wire coils and magnets

Electricity out

Collected heat energy is absorbed (taken up by) sodium, which passes it to water in a heat exchanger. As water boils into high-pressure steam, it blasts against and turns the angled blades of a turbine, which also spins the same main shaft of the generator.

21

FREE HEAT AT HOME

The Sun's heat, like its light, can be used in many ways. Millions of houses, schools, offices, and other buildings use solar heating for warmth and cooking.

PASSIVE SOLAR HEAT

Whenever sunlight hits an object, it not only lights it, but warms it as well — even on a cold winter day. This is called "passive" heating. A greenhouse is a very warm place because of all the light and heat rays that enter through the glass walls and roof. Darker objects also absorb much heat when in sunlight, while bright, shiny objects stay cooler. Passive solar heat is free and can be used to heat rooms or water.

Once solar-powered water heaters are installed, they are very durable and need almost no maintenance except occasional cleaning.

SOLAR HEATING

Water runs through pipes in the solar heating panel and absorbs the Sun's heat energy. The exchanger passes the heat to the hot water heater for bathing or room heating.

SUN'S RAYS

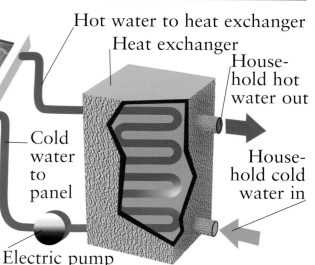

Hot water to heat exchanger

Heat exchanger

House-hold hot water out

Black, heat-absorbing pipes

Cold water to panel

House-hold cold water in

Heat-retaining glass cover

Solar roof panels help heat water.

Electric pump

THE SOLAR COOKER

The solar cooker and its stand are carefully turned to keep the mirror facing the Sun. The mirror's parabolic (curved bowl) shape helps it reflect almost all of the solar energy into one small area. On a sunny day, it can even boil water!

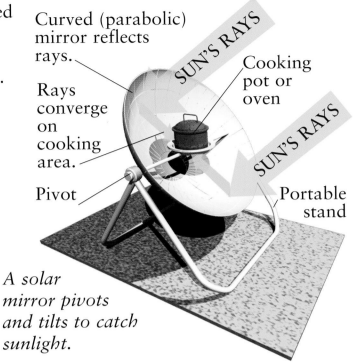

Curved (parabolic) mirror reflects rays.

Rays converge on cooking area.

SUN'S RAYS

Cooking pot or oven

SUN'S RAYS

Pivot

Portable stand

A solar mirror pivots and tilts to catch sunlight.

COOKING WITH MIRRORS

A solar stove is a simple device. Its curved mirror collects and reflects the Sun's infrared heat to cook the food. Solar power for cooking is especially useful in remote areas where no central power system is available. It is also very helpful in areas where fuel is scarce or if the people do not have spare money to spend on fuel.

Green ISSUES

It is easier and cheaper to store solar heat than solar-powered electricity. After solar heating equipment is installed and working, solar heating is free and causes no environmental harm. Solar cells must store their energy in expensive batteries.

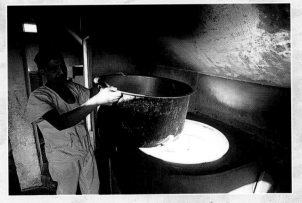

Sun-powered meal in India

NATURE'S SOLAR ENERGY

Almost all life on Earth relies on solar power. Plants capture the Sun's light energy to live and grow. Animals eat plants and are eaten by other animal predators — and on up through the food chain to humans.

PHOTOSYNTHESIS

Plants use a process called photosynthesis, which means "building with light." The plants grow and flower by using light from the Sun, carbon dioxide gas from air, and water from the soil to produce energy-rich substances called sugars.

A large tree has half a million leaves. They tilt and twist to face the Sun as it moves across the sky throughout the day.

THE LIVING SOLAR FACTORY

A plant leaf is a living solar factory. Its green substance, chlorophyll, absorbs light energy and converts it to chemical energy. This energy forms bonds, or links, between atoms (tiny particles) in the plant to produce glucose (a sugar).

In addition to light energy, photosynthesis requires two raw materials: water and carbon dioxide. Water flows through a plant's roots. Carbon dioxide passes into a plant's leaves through tiny holes, or pores, in a leaf's lower surface. Through photosynthesis, plants grow and produce oxygen that animals (and people!) need to stay alive.

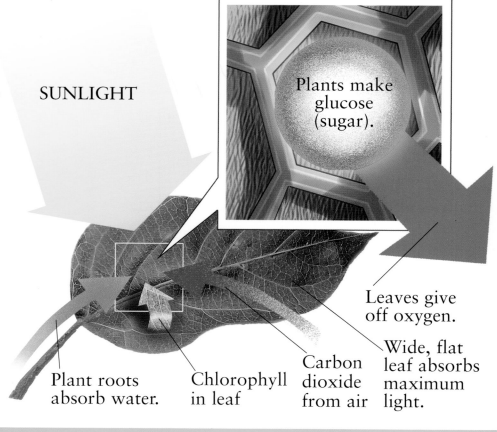

SUNLIGHT

Plants make glucose (sugar).

Leaves give off oxygen.

Wide, flat leaf absorbs maximum light.

Carbon dioxide from air

Chlorophyll in leaf

Plant roots absorb water.

24

FEEDING THE WORLD

Plants release their plentiful chemical energy when their sugars are broken apart into simple raw materials. The plant uses the energy to grow, repair itself, and to make seeds — which are actually little packets of stored energy in the form of proteins, starches, and oils. Scientists study photosynthesis to see if humans can develop technology that will mimic, or "copy," this form of solar power.

Solar energy passes from crops to plant-eaters (herbivores) such as cows — and on to humans.

ANCIENT SUNLIGHT

Oil (crude petroleum) is made into thousands of products, but the most familar are gasoline and diesel fuel. Oil's energy comes from solar energy trapped millions of years ago.

Flames from an oil rig are "prehistoric sunshine."

1) Tiny plant-like living organisms carried out photosynthesis, died, and sank; 2) More layers built up; 3) Layers were heated and squeezed deep in Earth's rocks; 4) Oil — "liquid fossil" formed (see also page 9).

SUNLIGHT

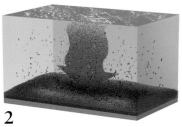

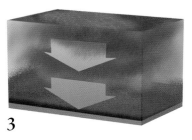

1

2

3

4

25

SECOND-HAND SOLAR

Plants are a rich store of trapped solar energy. Food produced by solar energy powers our bodies. Solar energy also drives our vehicles and machines.

BIOMASS ENERGY

Plants, animals, and other life-forms are known as biomass — "living matter." Their body substances contain chemical energy, gained secondhand from the Sun. Scientists have invented many ways to process different types of biomass for use as fuel.

The Hynol process mixes methane (natural gas) with organic matter — wood, leaves, animal droppings — at high temperatures and pressures to produce the high-energy liquid fuel methanol, or hydrogen gas.

BURNING FUELS

Numerous biomass products, ranging from wood and straw to dried animal dung are traditional heat sources for warmth and cooking. Rich oils from crops such as soy, sunflower, corn, and rapeseed (canola) can fuel specially adapted vehicle engines and even be used as an alternative fuel in power plants.

Burning any fuel produces carbon dioxide and other "greenhouse gases." Researchers believe that these gases trap solar heat in Earth's atmosphere, which causes global warming. As temperatures increase, worldwide climate changes occur. Food crops could fail and sea levels may rise to flood coastal cities.

BIOMASS TO BIOGAS

Garden clippings, food scraps, animal droppings, and vegetable peelings are put into the bio-fermenter. The biological (living) processes of rot, decay, and fermentation produce methane, the colorless, odorless gas we call natural gas. As the methane collects, it flows out through a pipe and can be burned as an energy source for cooking and heating, or in vehicle engines.

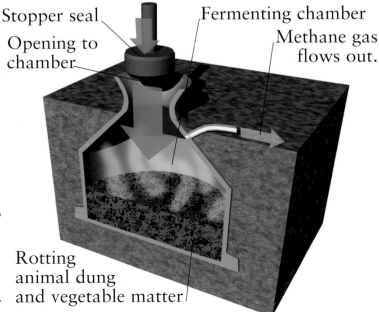

The bio-fermenter or bio-digester (right) acts like an enclosed compost heap. It produces methane gas, liquid methanol (left), or oils, such as soy oil, that can be used in vehicle engines.

Stopper seal

Opening to chamber

Fermenting chamber

Methane gas flows out.

Rotting animal dung and vegetable matter

27

SOLAR TAKE-OVER?

Right now, we harness very little of the solar energy around us, but the use of solar cells, panels, and arrays to heat and power our homes, appliances, and vehicles is increasing. Will solar power ever take over?

LOWER COSTS

Large-scale use of solar power, especially to produce electricity, has several drawbacks. It only works when the Sun shines, and storing it in batteries presents problems. Also, solar cells are quite costly to manufacture, so their electricity is expensive when compared to fossil-fuel power plants that burn traditional materials, such as coal, oil, and natural gas.

New solar cells are more than twice as efficient as older versions. Researchers continue to improve solar-cell energy output.

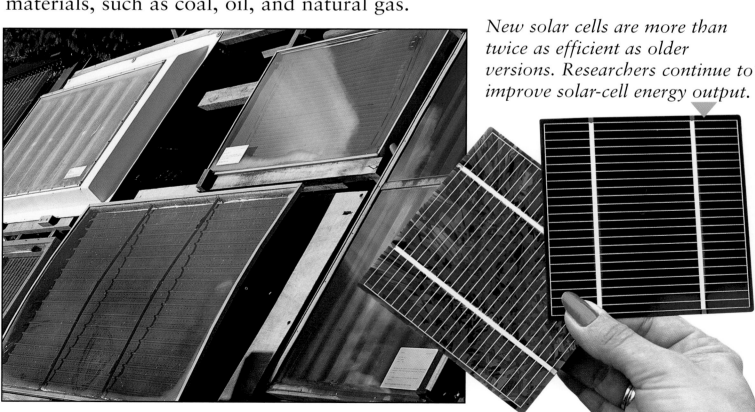

A "solar station" for electric vehicles works similar to a gasoline filling station. Solar-energy cars recharge when plugged into huge batteries powered by solar cells.

RUNNING OUT

Supplies of fossil fuels are running out, and burning these fuels causes pollution and global warming. Nuclear power also creates environmental hazards. Solar power, hydroelectricity (power from running water), and wind power cause less pollution and environmental harm and are sustainable or renewable. Another way we can stretch fuel supplies is by using less energy daily.

SOLAR CHIMNEY

A solar chimney combines the heat-catching glass of a greenhouse with the power of a wind turbine (below, left). An experimental solar chimney in Spain heats the ground and air under a vast glass roof. Hot air rising up the chimney spins a wind turbine that generates electricity. Are solar chimney "farms" (below, right) in our future?

FUTURE SOLAR ENERGY

Far above Earth, solar energy in space is powerful and constant. How can we capture it for use on Earth's surface?

ENERGY BEAMS

Giant solar panels orbiting Earth may someday convert solar light, heat, and other parts of the Sun's electromagnetic spectrum into a form of energy that we can use. One way to transport this energy back to Earth is through "energy beams," such as microwaves. For now, our solar power sources remain earthbound.

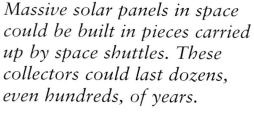

Massive solar panels in space could be built in pieces carried up by space shuttles. These collectors could last dozens, even hundreds, of years.

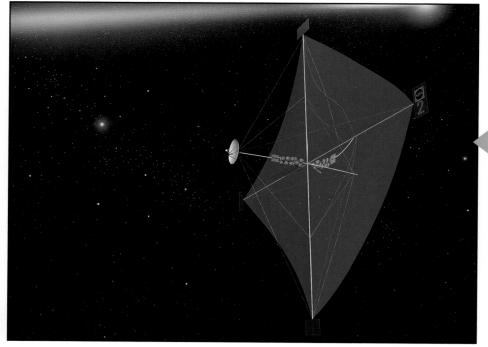

A solar space sail would be launched in a compact shape for unfolding into a solar panel once in orbit above Earth. Microwave-based energy beams might be used to transfer the solar power back to Earth. Careful aim of the beams is critical — they could "fry" or "destroy" the wrong target!

GLOSSARY

electromagnetic spectrum: the entire range of different wavelengths of energy generated by the Sun.

electrons: fast-moving parts of an atom that orbit its nucleus.

fission: the act of splitting atomic nuclei.

fusion: the act of combining atomic nuclei.

global warming: an increase in the average annual temperature around the world, thought to be caused by trapped atmospheric pollutants.

greenhouse gases: gases or vapors in the atmosphere that prevent the Sun's heat from escaping to outer space.

gravity: the one-way force that pulls two objects toward each other and varies in strength with object size and distance.

photosynthesis: the process green plants use to turn sunlight into growth.

photovoltaic cell: a device that uses light to produce power.

solar: having to do with the Sun.

sustainable: keeping something going.

turbine: a type of heavy machinery with fan-like, angled blades attached to a central shaft that spins when under pressure from wind or liquids.

MORE BOOKS TO READ

The Invention of the Silicon Chip: Revolution in Daily Life. Point of Impact (series). Windsor Chorlton (Heinemann Library)

Photosynthesis. Alvin Silverstein, Virginia Silverstein, Laura Silverstein (Millbrook Press)

Solar Power. Energy Forever (series). Ian S. Graham (Raintree/Steck Vaughn)

Solar Power of the Future: New Ways of Turning Sunlight into Energy. Library of Future Energy (series). Susan Jones (Rosen)

WEB SITES

Watch a short video on solar power.
www.nrel.gov/buildings/pv/learn2.html

Learn about the many aspects of solar energy.
www.sunwindsolar.com/a_solar/solar_energy_education.html

Due to the dynamic nature of the Internet, some web sites stay current longer than others. To find additional web sites, use a reliable search engine with one or more of the following keywords: *biomass, food chain,* Helios, *photosynthesis, photovoltaic, semiconductors, solar power, water cycle.*

INDEX

batteries 4, 10, 14, 15, 16, 29
bio-fermenter 27
biomass 8, 26–27

California 21
carbon dioxide 24, 27
chemical energy 9, 24–26
chlorophyll 24
coal 8, 15, 28

electromagnetic spectrum 6, 30
electrons 10, 30

fossil fuels 8, 9, 25, 28, 29

gamma rays 6
gas, natural 8, 15, 25, 26, 27, 28
generators 21, 31
global warming 27
gravity 9
greenhouse gases 15, 27

heat energy 9, 20–23
hydroelectricity 8, 9, 29
Hynol process 26

India 15, 23

infrared (heat) waves 6, 9, 20–23, 29

Japan 15

light, speed of 6

methane 26–27
methanol 26–27
microwaves 6, 30
Mojave Desert 13

Northumbria, University of 15
nuclear power 19, 29

oil 8, 15, 25, 28
oils, plant 25, 27
oxygen 24

photosynthesis 24
photovoltaic cells (see solar, cells)
plants 4, 7, 8, 9, 24–27
pollution 11, 29

radio waves 6, 27
radios 4, 14, 16, 17

satellites 6, 18, 19

solar
  arrays 10–11, 13, 16–17, 18, 28
  cells 5, 9, 10–11, 12–13, 15, 16, 17, 28
  chimney 29
  cooking 23
  energy, world map 12
  heating 9, 20–23
  panels 5, 10–14, 15, 16–17, 18, 19, 30
  power plants 9, 12–13, 14, 29
  sails 30
  watch 5, 16
space 5, 6, 18–19, 30
Spain 14
Sun, structure of 6–7
sustainable energy 7, 29

tidal energy 9
turbines 9, 21, 29

ultraviolet waves 6

water cycle 8–9, 12
winds 8, 9, 12, 29

X rays 6